SPRING

By Jeannine Gerkman

First published by Dog Ear Publishing
4011 Vincennes Rd
Indianapolis, IN 46268

This printing by Home-Heart Publishing
1025 Alameda de las Pulgas #817
Belmont, CA 94002 USA

This book is printed on acid-free paper.

Printed in the United States of America

Photo by Mark Gerece

Dedicated to:

FILOLI whose budding gardens inspired this poem

-and-

My parents and grandparents who gently

Instilled in me a love of reading and books early on in life

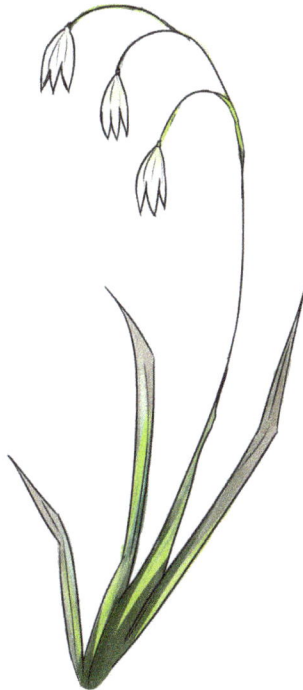

The days are getting warmer,

But
there's still
a faint chill

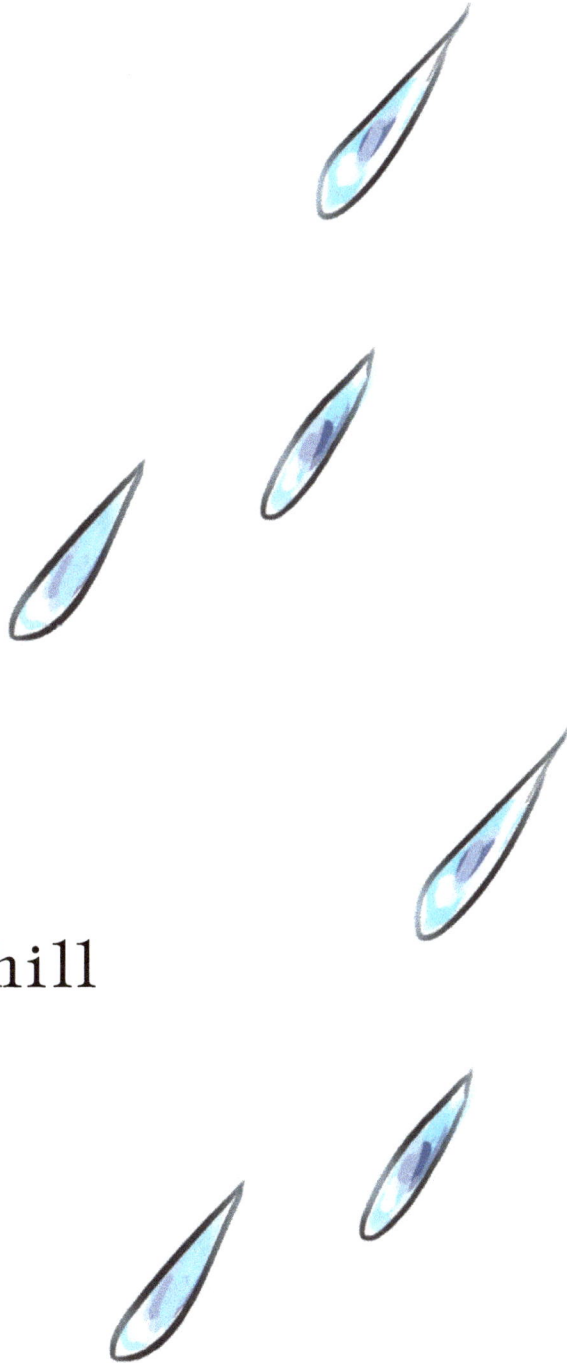

Rain has painted emerald

Every borough, tree and hill

Petals waft
like snowflakes

Onto arbors
and fronds

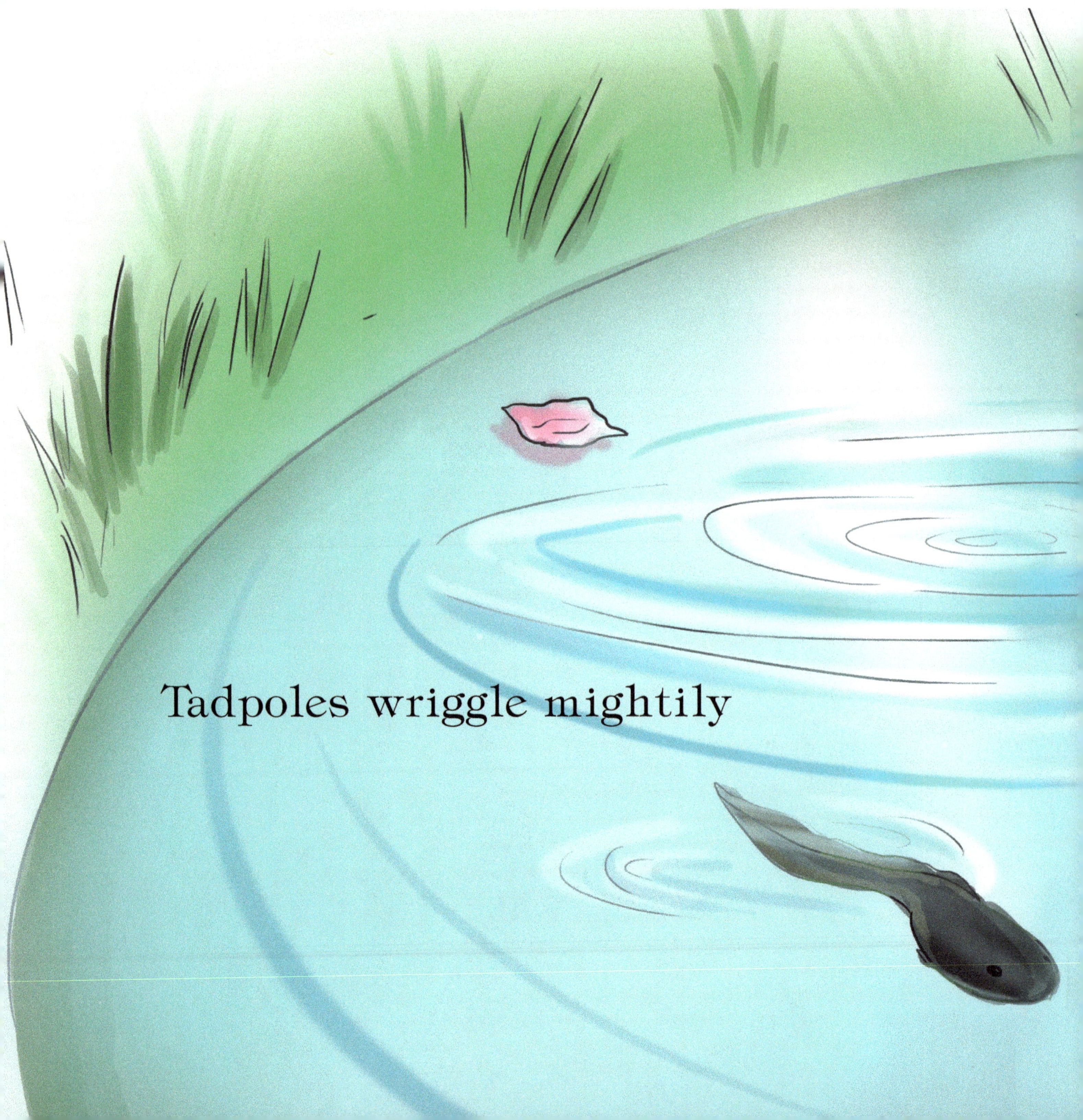

Tadpoles wriggle mightily

In shady, lazy ponds

Daffodils poke
their heads up,

Then gaze
at their feet

Tulips stand
in glory

And won't
admit defeat

Ducks quack
their welcome

To their newly hatched chicks

Egret, cormorant and swan

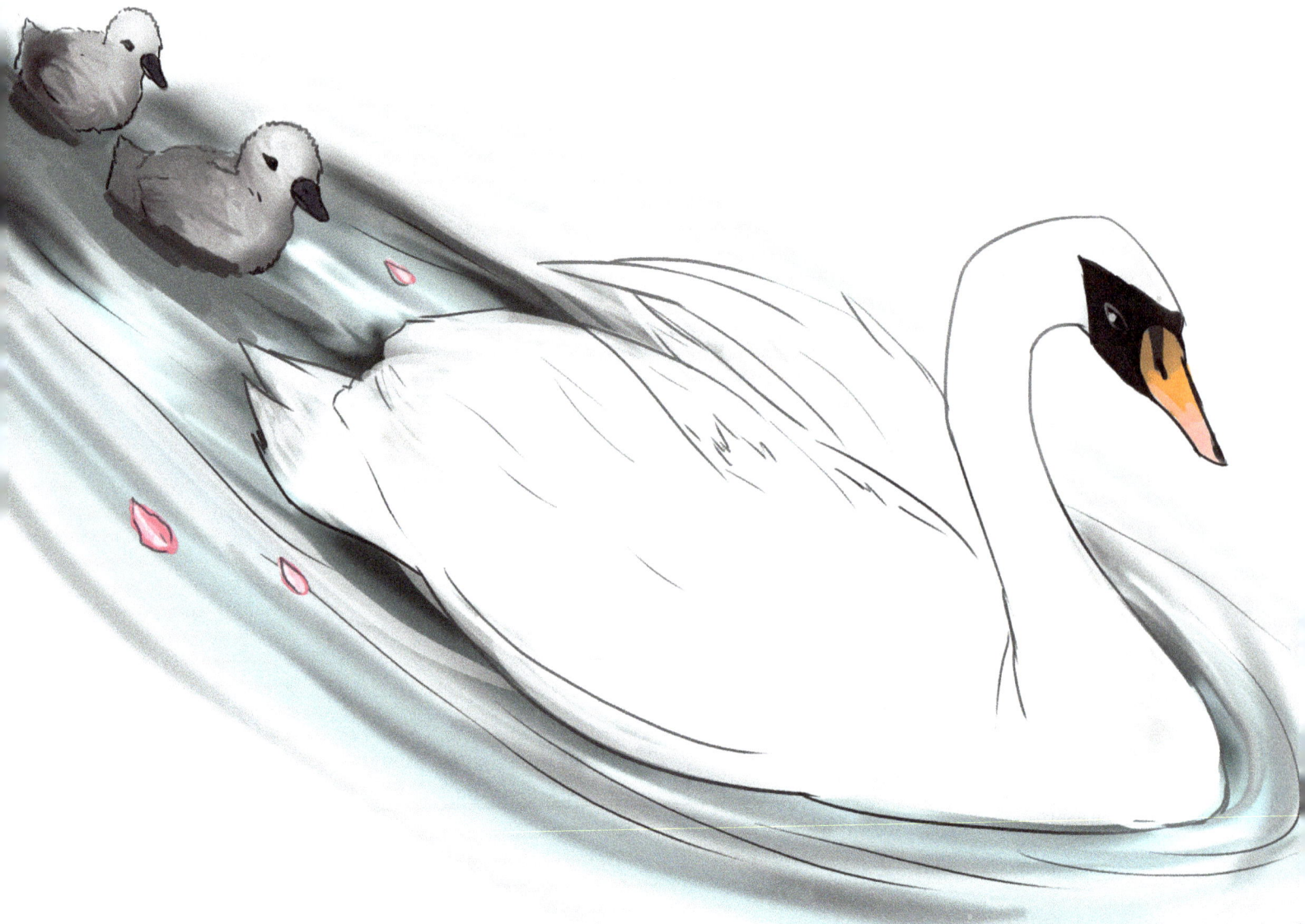

Add their chorus
to the mix

Fawn takes his first steps

Under Doe's watchful eye

Fledglings
spread
their wings

And learn
    how to fly

The sweet smell
of hyacinth

Competes with fresh mown lawn

Too soon, daylight hours will lengthen

And Spring will have gone.

Glossary:

Faint: Just a little, somewhat

Chill: A feeling of cold in the air

Emerald: Another word for green

Borough (brr-O): A group of houses in a neighborhood (nay-brr-hood)

Waft: Float gently in the breeze

Tadpole: In between a frog egg and a frog

Wriggle: Wiggle like a fish swims

Gaze: Look

Cormorant: Dark bird with a skinny neck that dives for fish

Chorus: Songs or calls done together as a group

Fledgling: In between a baby bird and an adult bird

Jeannine Gerkman moved to the Bay Area from the Pacific Northwest years ago and now lives with her husband in a home they built in Belmont, California. The oldest of six girls, she has written over 60 poems, some of them Award-winning. She's been a Realtor, banker, private chef, caregiver, volunteer, nanny, sister, auntie, great-auntie, nursing assistant and artist. She started composing rhyming verses to soothe her mother-in-law with Alzheimer's and found her poems give her and her listeners joy and contentment. She delights in word play and her favorite radio show is NPR's "Says You". Her next book: "Armadillos Amble" is an illustrated ABC book following 26 animals as they act using their matching letter, in alphabetical order... and it rhymes!

Here's a bonus poem and sneak peak at the upcoming book:

"Welcome to the alphabet
With this little song.
It's about some animals,
It isn't very long.
You can eye what they are doing
And listen with your ear.
Actions matching letters
You'll see it very clear.
So join me in this journey
From ambling A to zipping Z.
We'll laugh and copy actions,
Happy you and happy me."

Sign up to subscribe to her mailing list at www.home-heart.com
and/or follow her blog at AuthorPoetRealtor.blog

Armadillos Amble

Bears Browse

Camels Cuddle

Donkeys Drowse

...

www.ingramcontent.com/pod-product-compliance
Lightning Source LLC
Chambersburg PA
CBHW041600260326
41914CB00011B/1333